# Inheritance
## of
## Traits

## Why Is My Dog Bigger Than Your Dog?

Jen Green

Raintree

Chicago, Illinois

Edited by Adam Miller, Sian Smith, and Penny West
Designed by Philippa Jenkins
Original illustrations © Capstone Global Library Ltd 2014
Illustrated by Medi-mation
Picture research by Tracy Cummins
Originated by Capstone Global Library Ltd
Produced by Victoria Fitzgerald
Printed and bound in China by CTPS

17 16 15 14 13
10 9 8 7 6 5 4 3 2 1

**Library of Congress Cataloging-in-Publication Data**
Green, Jen, author.
  Inheritance of traits : why is my dog bigger than your dog? / Jen Green.
      pages cm.—(Show me science)
  Summary: "This fun book about dog shows teaches the core curriculum topic of inheritance."—Provided by publisher.
  Includes bibliographical references and index.
  ISBN 978-1-4329-8747-3 (hb)—ISBN 978-1-4329-8754-1 (pb)  1. Dogs—Breeding—Juvenile literature. 2. Dog shows—Juvenile literature. 3. Heredity—Juvenile literature. 4. Genetics—Juvenile literature.  I. Title.

  SF427.2.G74 2014
  636.7088—dc23         2013013102

**Acknowledgments**
The author and publisher are grateful to the following for permission to reproduce copyright material: Corbis p. 5 (© Ocean); Getty Images pp. 4 (New York Daily News Archive), 10 (John Mechalas), 11 (Abraham Cooper), 19 (Jane Burton), 20 (Joe Kohen), 26 (PAUL J. RICHARDS), 28 (Alexey Sokolov); Photo Researchers pp. 18 (Brian Evans), 23 (Addenbrookes Hospital / Science Source), 24 (William H. Mullins / Science Source); Shutterstock pp. 6 (© Artem Kursin), 8 (© ventdusud), 9 (© Pichugin Dmitry), 13 (© Cheryl Ann Quigley), 14 (© Anton Gvozdikov), 22 (© Linn Currie); Superstock pp. 7 (Biosphoto), 12 (Amiel / Photocuisine), 15 (Juniors), 16 (Juniors), 27 (Animals Animals).

Cover photograph of a Papillon and a Great Dane reproduced with permission of Corbis (© Don Mason).

We would like to thank Michael Bright for his invaluable help in the preparation of this book.

Some words are shown in bold, **like this**. You can find out what they mean by looking in the glossary.

# Welcome to the Show

Welcome to the Ultimate Pet Show—the world's best and biggest pet show. Here you can see pets of every kind, from pigeons to ponies. You plan to visit the dog, cat, and pony shows. On the way, you hope to find out about animal breeding and how **inheritance** works.

## Breeds and traits

Your first stop is the Ultimate Dog Show. Over a hundred **breeds** of dogs are on display here. A breed is a distinct type of dog with certain **traits** or features. For example, a Dalmatian has long legs, short hair, and a spotted coat. Over many years, these features have been developed through breeding.

At a dog show, thousands of dogs compete to win the top prize of Best in Show.

Genes are the reason that young animals, like this Basset Hound, look like their parents.

## Genes and inheritance

Dogs, cats, ponies, and all living things pass on features to their **offspring**. This process is called inheritance or **heredity**. Inheritance happens because of tiny structures called **genes**. Genes control features such as the length and color of a dog's hair. Genes are the reason dogs give birth to puppies and cats give birth to kittens, not the other way around!

## What are genes?

Genes are found inside **cells**—the tiny units that make up an animal's body. When animals reproduce (have young), genes work like a master plan or blueprint. They form a set of instructions that control how the babies develop.

# The World of Dogs

At the Ultimate Dog Show, you can see dogs of all sizes. There are huge Great Danes, chunky Saint Bernards, and tiny Chihuahuas. A big, heavy Saint Bernard may weigh a hundred times more than a Chihuahua!

## Same but different

As you wander around, you notice that dogs vary in shape as well as size. For example, Afghan Hounds are tall and long-legged, with long noses and long, silky fur. Pugs are small and stocky, with snubbed noses and short fur. Despite these differences, all dogs belong to the same **species**—the **domestic** dog.

This Chihuahua is many times smaller than this Mastiff.

## LITTLE AND LARGE

Great Danes and Irish Wolfhounds are the tallest dogs, standing up to 39 inches (1 meter) at the shoulder. Saint Bernards are the heaviest dogs, weighing up to 200 pounds (90 kilograms). At the other end of the scale, the tiny Chihuahua stands only 8 inches (20 centimeters) tall, and may weigh just 2 pounds (1 kilogram).

## Different jobs

Different **breeds** of dog have been developed to do different work. Border Collies were bred to herd sheep. Sporting dogs, such as Labradors, were developed to retrieve animals shot by hunters. Hounds, with their excellent sense of smell, were bred to track prey such as deer. Fierce-looking Mastiffs were developed as guard dogs. Small or "toy" dogs were originally bred as hot water bottles, to keep their owners warm!

Dachshunds come in long-haired, wire-haired, and smooth-haired varieties.

# Ancient Breeds

You reach an area where some of the world's oldest dog **breeds** are on show. You stop to look at a Siberian Husky. These dogs were developed many centuries ago to pull sleds in the Arctic. With its thick fur and powerful build, the Siberian Husky looks a lot like the **ancestor** of all dogs, the wolf.

## How did dogs develop?

You stop by a display screen that explains the connection between dogs and wolves. It says **domestic** dogs have been around for at least 12,000 years. The ancestors of modern dogs were probably young, hungry wolves that entered hunters' camps in search of food. The hunters tamed the animals and discovered they could be used to help with hunting or to guard the camp.

Siberian Huskies, shown here, and German Shepherds look similar to wolves.

Cave paintings like this one from North Africa show that dogs have helped humans for thousands of years.

Over the next few thousand years, domestic dogs developed. But all these dogs were not alike. Some were fast and good at tracking. Others were fierce and made good guard dogs. Others were small and cuddly. All the breeds of dog that we know today developed from these beginnings.

## The dog family

Wolves and domestic dogs are members of the family of doglike animals called canines. Jackals and wild dogs belong to the same family. Foxes are also related. All canines are meat-eating hunters, with strong legs and sharp teeth to outrun and kill their prey.

You reach a section where Greyhounds are on show. You study a Greyhound's lean, muscular body and watch a video about Greyhound racing, which shows the dogs speeding around a racetrack. With its long head and neck, flexible body, and powerful legs, every part of a Greyhound's body is built for speed.

## Selective breeding

The Greyhound **breed** was developed over many years through a process called **selective breeding**. Breeders selected (chose) their very fastest, strongest animals to breed from. Over time, the breed became even stronger and faster, with animals reaching record speeds. Modern Greyhounds can run at up to 45 miles (72 kilometers) per hour over a short distance.

Greyhounds are born with a natural instinct and ability to run.

# Born to run

Greyhounds are an ancient breed. These dogs were developed over 4,000 years ago to hunt antelope. Later they were bred for track racing.

For centuries, breeders selected animals without understanding how **inheritance** worked. Now we know that features pass from parents to their young through **genes**, which are found inside **cells**. In the late 1800s, the development of powerful microscopes allowed scientists to see inside cells for the first time. This was a big step toward the discovery of genes.

# The Ultimate Pony Show

You feel like taking a break from the dog show and head off to the Ultimate Pony Show. The show includes horses of different sizes, from large, heavy draft horses to small Shetland ponies. Their coats vary in color from black to chestnut, gray, white, and golden. Some horses have spotty or piebald (patchy) markings.

## Taming wild horses

There are over a hundred horse **breeds**, all descended from wild horses that galloped over the plains of Asia about 6,000 years ago. As horses were tamed, people noticed that they could be useful in many ways. They could carry soldiers into battle and pull carts or chariots.

In some parts of the world, horses are still used to pull farm equipment.

Some horses are bred for sports such as polo, racing, and show-jumping.

## Developing horse breeds

Over time, different breeds of horses were developed to do different jobs. Some were bred to carry riders. Others were bred to pull coaches and carriages. Draft horses were developed to haul plows and other farm equipment. A farmer breeding draft horses would select his biggest and strongest horses to breed from. A breeder might also **mate** a strong horse with a fast one, to get a foal (baby horse) with both speed and strength.

## The variety of horses

The smallest pony is the Falabella, which stands just 30 inches (75 centimeters) tall at the shoulder. The largest draft horses stand over 70 inches (180 centimeters) tall and weigh over 2,200 pounds (1,000 kilograms).

# The World of Cats

The Ultimate Cat Show is in the next hall. You marvel at the variety of **breeds** on show. All **domestic** cats are descended from tabby-colored African wildcats. Cats were kept as pets in ancient Egypt over 3,500 years ago. They helped Egyptian farmers by killing rats and mice.

## A variety of cats

Looking around, you see that cats vary in shape and color, just as dogs and horses do. You stop to admire a Persian, with its long, fluffy fur and flattish face. Not far away, Siamese cats are on show. They have short fur and longer noses. There are cats with long, fluffy tails, short tails, and Manx cats with no tails at all!

Cats vary in color
from black to gray,
white, cream,
orange, and tabby.

# THE CAT FAMILY

The domestic cat belongs to the cat family, which has 37 **species**. The family is divided into big cats and small cats. Big cats include the lion, tiger, and leopard. Ocelots, servals, and wildcats are small cats.

## Natural skills and instincts

Whether large or small, all cats have similar body shapes. They also share certain instincts and abilities. All cats are strong, agile, and good at climbing. They have very good senses, especially sight. All cats are meat-eating hunters. Hunting is a natural instinct, even in pet cats. All these qualities pass from parents to their young through **genes**.

The cat's natural hunting ability is used by farmers to control mice.

# How Do Genes Work?

You stop by a breeder who is showing two prize-winning cats—a male and a female. A sign says either animal can be rented for breeding. You talk to the breeder, who explains about **inheritance** and **genes**.

This prize-winning cat is a Maine Coon **breed**.

CAT SHOW WINNER

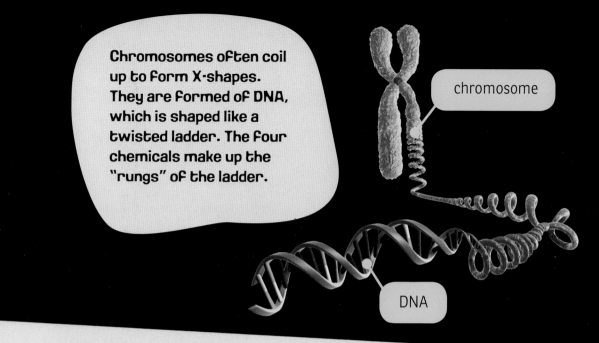

Chromosomes often coil up to form X-shapes. They are formed of DNA, which is shaped like a twisted ladder. The four chemicals make up the "rungs" of the ladder.

chromosome

DNA

## All about genes

Genes are found in the **cell nucleus**—the tiny blob that acts as the cell's control center. Genes are sections of long strands called **chromosomes**. Each chromosome carries thousands of genes. Each gene is like a small snippet of information, carrying the instructions for a particular feature, such as fur color. The full set of instructions works like a blueprint to build new baby animals, such as puppies, kittens, and foals.

Genes are made of chemicals called **DNA**. DNA has four special chemicals that are arranged in different ways. Just as the letters of the alphabet can be arranged to spell words, so the arrangement of the chemicals forms a code. The code tells cells how to work and develop.

## NUMBERS OF CHROMOSOMES

Different types of animals have different numbers of chromosomes in their cells. Cats have 38 chromosomes, dogs have 78, and horses have 64. Humans have 46 chromosomes. The actual number is not very important, but the number is always even because chromosomes come in pairs.

# Puppies and Kittens

You head back toward the dog show. On your way, you pass a pen with a female cat and her litter of kittens. Nearby is a display that explains how animals reproduce (have young).

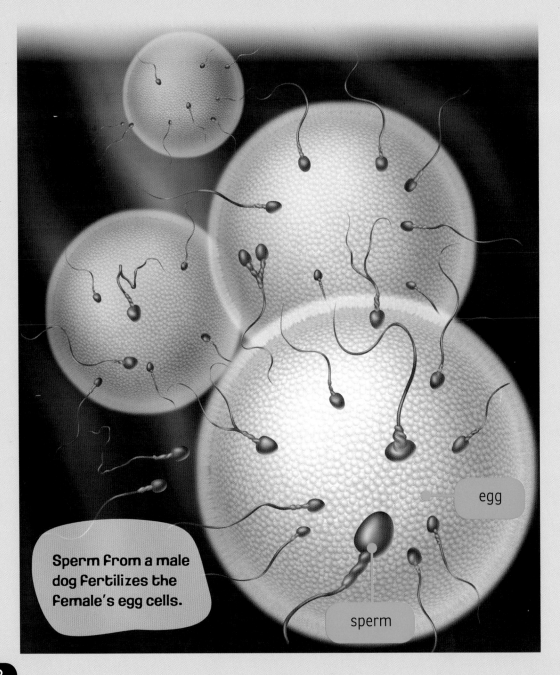

Sperm from a male dog fertilizes the female's egg cells.

egg

sperm

A female tabby cat feeds her kittens milk.

# New life

Dogs, cats, and horses are **mammals**. Humans are also mammals. In all mammals, reproduction begins when a male **mates** with a female. New life starts when a sex **cell** from the male, called **sperm**, joins with the female's egg cell. This moment is called **fertilization**. In all mammals, fertilization happens inside the mother. The baby develops in a space called the **womb**.

The fertilized cell divides many times to form a ball of cells that slowly develops into a baby. As more cells are made, **genes** instruct the cells to develop into different types, which eventually form different body parts. When the baby is fully developed, it is born.

# Gestation and litter sizes

Mammals give birth to different numbers of young. In each case, the babies spend a certain time developing inside the mother. This time is called **gestation**. Both dogs and cats give birth after about 9 weeks. A female dog may have between 1 and 12 puppies, while a cat may have up to 10 kittens. Foals spend 11 months in gestation. Usually only one foal is born, but sometimes there are twins.

# Best in Show

Back at the dog show, some classes have been judged. A Beagle wins first prize. Show dogs often have long, odd-sounding names. The winner's name is Sophie III Amazing Trick of Hounslow. Her owners call her Trixie for short!

## A full set of genes

You talk to the breeder, who explains that Trixie was bred from two prize-winning dogs. Their names were Clever Trick of Hounslow and Sophie II Amazing Lady. Trixie's full name reflects her parentage, but the breeder explains that she got more than her name from her parents. She also inherited half her **genes** from her mother and half from her father.

# First steps

Some newborn **mammals** are more helpless than others. Newborn puppies and kittens are weak and cannot stand. Their eyes are closed, so they cannot see. Within two weeks their eyes open and they start to crawl around. Foals are able to stand on their long, wobbly legs just an hour after birth. After a few hours, they can run!

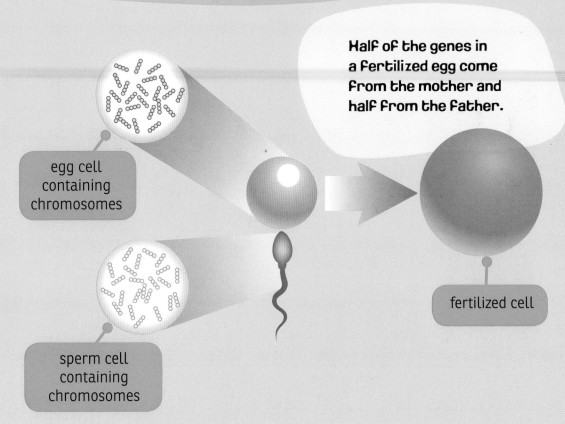

Half of the genes in a fertilized egg come from the mother and half from the father.

egg cell containing chromosomes

sperm cell containing chromosomes

fertilized cell

How does this **inheritance** happen? Well, you remember that dogs have 78 **chromosomes** in almost all of their **cells**. However, sex cells (**sperm** and egg) are different. They only contain half the normal number of chromosomes—39 chromosomes in dogs. When the sperm joins with the egg, it forms the full set of 78 chromosomes that are needed to build a puppy like Trixie.

# Brother and Sister

The breeder is also showing a brother and sister pair, named Reggie and Ellie. You notice that brother and sister look similar, but their faces and markings are slightly different. If the two dogs come from the same litter, and inherited half their **genes** from each parent, why don't they look exactly the same?

These prize-winning dogs are related, but have different markings.

# Variation

For centuries, breeders have known that within each **generation** of young that is born, some animals are slightly different. For example, one puppy might have slightly longer ears than normal. These differences, called **variations**, happen naturally. If breeders like the variation, they choose that animal to breed from. In this way, the feature becomes more common. Variation allows **breeds** to change over time.

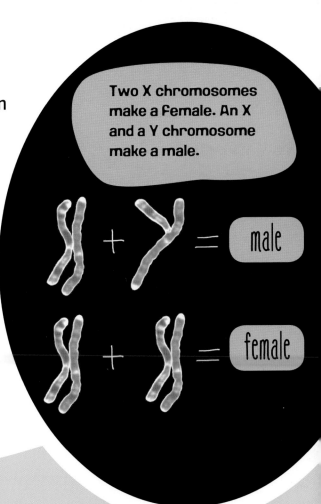

Two X chromosomes make a female. An X and a Y chromosome make a male.

male

female

## Changing places

Puppies in a litter have similar, but not identical, genes. This is because when sex **cells** are made, some of the genes change places. Each **sperm** cell and each egg cell contains a different selection of genes. When the sex cells join, there is a different combination every time.

## Boy or girl?

What makes some puppies male and others female? This is decided by a pair of **chromosomes** called sex chromosomes. The mother's egg always has an X chromosome, half the code for a female. The father's sperm may contain an X or a Y chromosome. If the sperm adds another X, the puppy will be female. If it adds a Y, the puppy will be male.

# The Odd Puppy Out

You stop by a pen that holds a black Labrador with her litter of four puppies. The proud father, another black Labrador, is nearby. But wait! You notice that one of the puppies is brown! How can two black dogs produce a brown puppy?

Genes have decided the color of these puppies.

## Strong and weak genes

You ask the owner, who reminds you that **genes** come in pairs. One of the pair comes from each parent, but both control the same feature, such as hair color. In Labradors, the gene for black hair is stronger than the gene for brown hair. We call the strong gene **dominant** and the weak gene **recessive**. If one dog passes on the black-hair gene and the other passes on the brown-hair gene, the puppy will be black.

If two black dogs with one black-hair gene and one brown-hair gene **mate** and have several puppies, the chances are that one puppy will be brown. This puppy has received the brown-hair gene from both the father's **sperm** and the mother's egg.

## Gregor Mendel

In the 1860s, Austrian scientist Gregor Mendel experimented with **heredity** by breeding pea plants. Mendel crossed plants producing violet flowers with ones producing white flowers and got only plants with violet flowers. However, when he bred the new violet-flowered plants together, he got some plants that produced white flowers. He realized that the violet flower color was strong and the white flower color was weak. It was not until many years later that scientists discovered the colors were controlled by strong and weak genes.

# Champion Sniffers

You head across to the central show ring to watch a display of sniffer dogs. These dogs are trained to use their excellent sense of smell. They are used in police work to sniff out explosives, track criminals by scent, and find people lost in the wild.

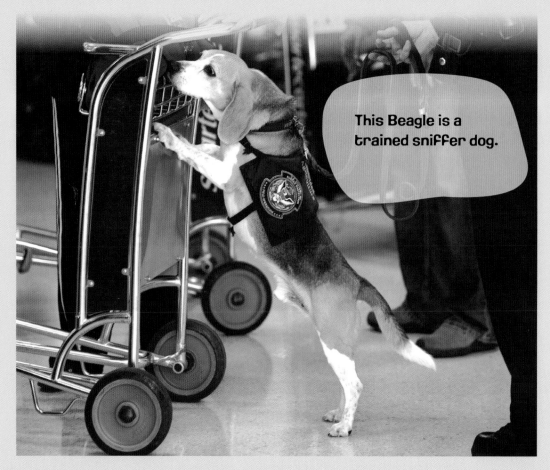

This Beagle is a trained sniffer dog.

## Training and performance

You watch as a dog sniffs out a hidden package. The dog has inherited its excellent sense of smell and the instinct to sniff things out. But years of training have increased its tracking skills. Training has also strengthened the bond between the dog and its owner, so it is able to obey different commands and carry out a range of tasks.

A Bloodhound's nose is a thousand times more sensitive than a human's.

**Genes** play a big part in any dog's appearance. For example, they determine its size and the shapes of its body parts, such as its legs, ears, nose, and tail. However, diet and exercise also affect how a dog looks. Dogs that are given too much food can become overweight. Not enough food makes a dog thin. Exercise increases a dog's stamina (staying power) and strengthens its muscles, so it can run for longer without getting tired.

## The work of sniffer dogs

Sniffer dogs are trained to find people buried in the ruins of buildings after an earthquake. In snowy mountains, they find people buried by avalanches. Many different types of dogs are used as sniffer dogs.

# The World's Best-Trained Dog

As the show ends, an agility contest takes place outside. The dogs have to complete an obstacle course—jumping hurdles, weaving between poles, going up and down stairs, and crawling through a tunnel. The winner is the dog that finishes fastest without making any mistakes.

**Inheritance**, experience, and training all play a part in agility contests.

## Training matters

You watch the dogs run the course—they are amazing! Following their owner's shouts, whistles, and signals, they twist and turn to take the obstacles in the right order. As with the sniffer dogs, training has built on the dog's natural abilities and instincts.

## Training pays off

The winner receives his prize. Wolfie is a crossbreed, a German Shepherd-Greyhound cross. The dog combines the best qualities of both **breeds**. Greyhounds are very fast, while German Shepherds are strong, clever, and easy to train. Breeders often cross two breeds to get a champion in classes, such as agility contests, in which any dog can take part. Wolfie's name reflects his proud **ancestor**, the wolf!

# Mixed-breed dogs

Dog shows are fun to watch, but **pedigree** or purebred dogs sometimes suffer from health problems. This is because breeders have only a small number of pedigree dogs to choose from if they want to breed a champion. Health problems, as well as good qualities, can be passed on in **genes**. Mixed-breed dogs (mongrels) are often healthier than purebreed ones. They usually live longer. So a mixed breed is a great choice if you want a dog.

**ancestor** animal or person that an animal or person is descended from. The wolf is the ancestor of all domestic dogs.

**breed** small group within a species of animal

**cell** tiny unit that all living things are made out of

**chromosome** x-shaped structure found inside nucleus of a cell, which contains genes

**DNA** strings of chemicals inside cells that make up genes and form a code

**domestic** tame

**dominant** describes a gene that is strong and controls an inherited feature

**fertilization** moment when a male sex cell joins with a female egg, to start a new life

**generation** all the animals (or people) born and living at one time

**genes** sections of DNA that controls an inherited feature, such as eye or hair color

**gestation** time between fertilization and birth, when a female animal is pregnant

**heredity** process through which features are passed on from parents to their young, also called inheritance

**inheritance** see heredity

**mammal** member of the group of animals with hair on their bodies, whose young feed on their mother's milk

**mate** when animals come together in order to have young

**nucleus** tiny dot at the center of a cell, which controls how the cell works

**offspring** young of an animal

**pedigree** purebred animal that belongs to a recognized breed

**recessive** describes a gene that is weaker than a strong, or dominant, gene

**selective breeding** when a breeder chooses a particular animal to breed from because the animal has features that the breeder wants the offspring to have

**species** kind of living thing; members of a species can breed to make more members

**sperm** male sex cell

**trait** certain feature that an animal has

**variation** change or difference

**womb** space inside a female mammal in which the baby develops

# Find Out More

## Books

Claybourne, Anna. *The Usborne Introduction to Genes and DNA*. Tulsa, Okla.: EDC, 2003.

Clutton-Brock, Juliet. *Dog* (Eyewitness). New York: DK, 2004.

Green, Jen. *Inheritance and Reproduction* (Essential Life Science). Chicago: Heinemann Library, 2014.

Parker, Steve. *In Your Genes: Reproduction and Heredity* (Body Talk). Chicago: Raintree, 2006.

## Web sites

**www.amnh.org/explore/ology/genetics**
The web site for the American Museum of Natural History has lots of information about genetics.

**kidshealth.org/kid/talk/qa/what_is_gene.html**
This web site has simple explanation of genes and inheritance.

**pbskids.org/dragonflytv/games/game_dogbreeding.html**
Have fun with this genetics game. Try your hand breeding various types of Border Collie puppies.

**www.sciencekidsathome.com/science_topics/genetics-a.html**
There is another simple explanation of how genes work on this web site.

## Places to visit

The American Museum of
  Natural History
Central Park West
79th Street
New York, New York 10024
**www.amnh.org**

The Museum of Science
  and Industry
5700 Lake Shore Drive
Chicago, IL 60637
**www.msichicago.org**

# Index

# JUDITH CASELEY

# Witch
# MAMA

Greenwillow Books, New York

Watercolor paints, colored pencils, and a black pen were used
for the full-color art. The text type is Souvenir Medium.
Copyright © 1996 by Judith Caseley
Greenwillow Books, a division of William Morrow & Company, Inc.,
1350 Avenue of the Americas, New York, NY 10019.
Printed in Singapore by Tien Wah Press
First Edition 10  9  8  7  6  5  4  3  2  1

Library of Congress Cataloging-in-Publication Data
Caseley, Judith.
Witch mama / by Judith Caseley.
p.      cm.
Summary: Jenna celebrates her Halloween birthday
by trick-or-treating with her younger brother in the
neighborhood and going to a party at school where
her mother gives her a special surprise.
ISBN 0-688-14457-8 (trade)
ISBN 0-688-14458-6 (lib. bdg.)
[1. Halloween—Fiction.      2. Mothers and
daughters—Fiction.      3. Brothers and
sisters—Fiction.]      I. Title.
PZ7.C2677Wi      1996      [E]—dc20
95-35847      CIP      AC

**To my own sweet Mama,**
**with love**

Jenna was born on Halloween day.
"You were two weeks early, and I was dressed up
like a big, fat witch," Mama told Jenna.
"And Daddy called you Witch Mama!" said Jenna.
"When you arrived," said Mama, "Daddy called
you his little sandwitch."

Jenna's friends thought she was
lucky because she always got to go
trick-or-treating on her birthday.

On Halloween morning Jenna woke up and called out, "Witch Mama, make me my breakfast!" Mama laughed the best witch cackle that she could muster and made oats in mud for Jenna's breakfast, which was really cereal in chocolate milk.

Jenna's brother, Mickey, wasn't used to Witch Mama at breakfast. He covered his ears when Mama cackled, and said, "No."

"It's only Witch Mama," Jenna told him.

After school Jenna put on her Little Bo Peep
costume. She carried Mickey's toy sheep and
a shepherd's crook.

Mama dressed Mickey like a clown, but when
she tried to paint round red cheeks on his face,
he shook his head and said, "No."
He let Jenna paint his nose blue.

So a blue-nosed clown and Little Bo Peep rang the neighborhood doorbells, shouting "Trick or treat!" When a door opened, Jenna held out her bag, and Mickey hid behind her until Jenna said, "Hold out your bag, too, honey."

Jenna smiled when fat candy bars plopped to the bottom. The jingle of pennies made Mickey laugh.

Mrs. Pringle threw a fig bar into their bags, and
when Mickey made a face, Jenna whispered,
"You have lots of chocolate already."
Mr. Levy dropped in a rubber bat, and Jenna
told Mickey, "That's not for eating."

Mickey rang Mrs. Pidgeon's doorbell all by himself.
The door flew open and spooky music started and a
ghost floated to the doorway, and Mickey hid behind
Mama until she had blue nose paint all over her jacket.
"It's really Mrs. Pidgeon," whispered Jenna to Mickey.
"How's your broken arm?" Mama asked.
"Not too bad," said Mrs. Pidgeon, waving good-bye
with the arm that was in the cast.

When trick-or-treating was over, Mama took away all the unwrapped candy. Jenna picked out four chocolate candy bars, and Mama stuck a candle in each one.

Papa came home, and they sang "Happy Birthday to You!"

Then Mama and Jenna and Papa and Mickey ate their candy bars, and it was time for the Halloween party at Jenna's school. This year Mama was helping. Jenna asked Mama what she was going to do.

"It's a surprise," said Mama.

Then Mama remembered Jenna's birthday present, and Jenna unwrapped the box and took out a pair of big pumpkin earrings.

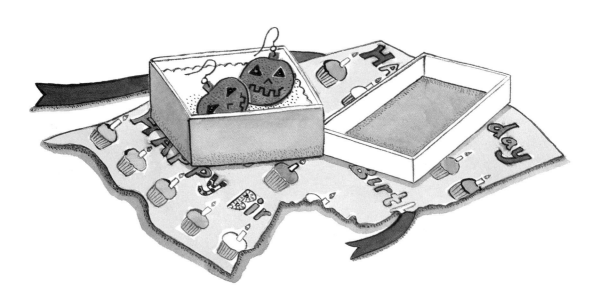

"I love them!" said Jenna, but Little Bo Peeps
don't wear pumpkin earrings, so she let Mama
wear them to the Halloween party.

Mama left early, and a little while later Papa and Jenna and Mickey walked to school together. They joined a line of ghouls and witches and mermaids and robots and princesses.

At the school entrance Jenna's friends came running.
"Wait until you see the Haunted Hallway," they told
her. "It's the greatest!"
Everyone pointed to a tunnel in the corridor
made out of sheets and clotheslines.
A sign in front said "Haunted Hallway.
Enter at your own risk!"

But the line in the hallway was much too long,
so Jenna and Mickey went to the gym instead.
They tossed rings onto pegs and won bags of
candy corn. They threw balls into fishbowls
and won skeleton necklaces.

They marched in the costume parade, out in the pitch-black playground, with their flashlights waving.

**Haunted HALLWAY~**
Enter at your own risk!

"Where's Mama?" said Jenna afterward.

"Where's Mama?" said Mickey.

Papa asked around, and everyone pointed
to the Haunted Hallway.

"We're in luck," said Papa. "The line is
shorter." And he waved them in.

Jenna took Mickey's hand, and they started
walking. Scary music was playing, and bats
were flying.

"No," said Mickey, planting his feet.

"The bats are made of paper," whispered
Jenna. "And the electric fan is making them
fly." She pulled Mickey. "Let's find Mama."

A bandaged mummy pointed a finger. "All the
way back," moaned a low voice.
"No," said Mickey.
"It's Mrs. Pidgeon again," whispered Jenna.
"See the cast on her arm?"

"Keep going," yowled a white-faced ghoul.

"No," said Mickey.

"It's Mr. Finn," said Jenna. "He yells like that
in the playground."

Frankenstein's monster raised his arms in the air.

Mickey tried to hide behind Jenna.

"It's the crossing guard," said Jenna. "Can't you see his moustache?"

She dragged Mickey until they reached a long wooden box with some witchy boots sticking out the end of it.

Jenna and Mickey took baby steps forward.

"It's a coffin," whispered Jenna. She leaned over the box.
A pale green face with a big, hairy mole on it peered back
at her. "Hello, Jenna and Michael," said a witchy voice.

"No," said Mickey, covering his eyes.

"Look!" said Jenna. "Look at her ears!"

Mickey peeked. Swinging from the witch's green-colored
ears were Jenna's big pumpkin birthday earrings.

"It's Mama," said Jenna. "Witch Mama!"

"Yes!" said Mickey.

Mama and Jenna and Mickey started laughing.
Then Mama kissed them both, and they left the
haunted hallway with green lipstick prints on
their cheeks.